QUESTIONING FOR TEACHING & LEARNING

QUESTIONING FOR TEACHING & LEARNING

{ Kate Jones }

Sage

1 Oliver's Yard
55 City Road
London EC1Y 1SP

2455 Teller Road
Thousand Oaks
California 91320

10th Floor, Emaar Capital Tower 2
MG Road, Sikanderpur, Sector 26
Gurugram, Haryana – 122002
India

8 Marina View Suite 43-053
Asia Square Tower 1
Singapore 018960

Editor: Amy Thornton
Senior project editor: Chris Marke
Cover design: Wendy Scott
Typeset by: C&M Digitals (P) Ltd, Chennai, India

© 2026 Kate Jones

Apart from any fair dealing for the purposes of research or private study, or criticism or review, as permitted under the Copyright, Designs and Patents Act 1988, this publication may be reproduced, stored or transmitted in any form, or by any means, only with the prior permission in writing of the publishers, or in the case of reprographic reproduction, in accordance with the terms of licences issued by the Copyright Licensing Agency. Enquiries concerning reproduction outside those terms should be sent to the publishers.

Library of Congress Control Number: 2025943505

British Library Cataloguing in Publication Data

A catalogue record for this book is available from the British Library

ISBN 978-1-0362-3091-3 (pbk)

CONTENTS

About this book vii
About the series ix
About the author xi
Introduction xiii

1 **Questioning: 'know thy purpose'** 1

2 **Question banks for teaching and learning** 13

3 **Alternatives to 'hands up'** 21

4 **Retrieval practice** 35

5 **Multiple-choice questions** 45

6 **Questioning: Mix it up!** 57

Afterword 73
References 75
Index 79

{ ABOUT THIS BOOK }

A Little Guide for Teachers: Questioning for Teaching and Learning offers practical advice for teachers on using questioning in the classroom to maximise opportunities for teaching and learning. It is linked to research evidence for the effectiveness of questioning as a teaching tool, equipping teachers to improve their questioning techniques, develop oracy skills in their learners and enhance the consolidation and recall of learning.

- Authored by experts in the field
- Easy to dip in-and-out of
- Interactive activities encourage you to write into the book and make it your own
- Fun engaging illustrations throughout
- Read in an afternoon or take as long as you like with it!

Find out more at
www.sagepub.co.uk/littleguides

{ ABOUT THE SERIES }

A LITTLE GUIDE FOR TEACHERS series is little in size but big on all the support and inspiration you need to navigate your day-to-day life as a teacher.

 CASE STUDY

 REFLECTION

 NOTE THIS DOWN

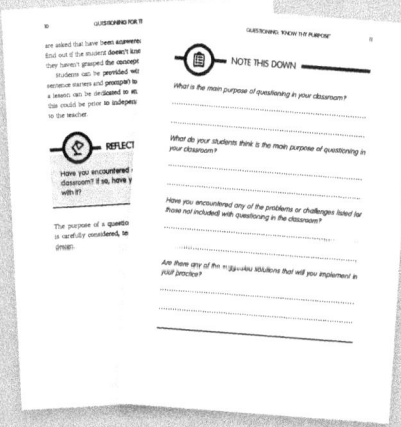

www.sagepub.co.uk/littleguides

ABOUT THE AUTHOR

Kate Jones is an experienced teacher, leader, bestselling author, blogger and award-winning international speaker.

As a secondary history teacher, Kate has taught in the United Kingdom and in British curriculum schools in the United Arab Emirates. She is currently Senior Associate for Teaching and Learning at Evidence Based Education and delivers training and support to schools across the UK and internationally. In addition to this, Kate is the author of ten books including a bestselling series on retrieval practice.

Kate was the editor of *The researchED Guide to Cognitive Science*, published in 2023, and her latest book *Feedback: Strategies to Support Teacher Workload and Improve Pupil Progress* (2024) focused on evidence-informed and workload-friendly feedback strategies to support teacher workload and student progress.

Kate writes extensively about education in various educational magazines including *Teach Middle East* and the *TES* and is the founder of the 'Love to Teach Podcast'. She has presented as keynote speaker at various events and conferences around the world including in Chile, Hong Kong, the United States of America, Sri Lanka, Dubai and more.

INTRODUCTION

Questioning takes place in every classroom, every lesson, every day. Questioning is at the heart of effective teaching and learning. Despite the importance of questioning, it has often been overlooked in professional development. Questioning can be taken for granted as something that teachers simply do naturally and instinctively (this is a risky approach to take!). Questioning in the classroom is too important to leave to chance.

The *purpose* of questioning can vary depending on the age, key stage and subject-specific context, as explored in Chapter 1. This chapter also includes some potential problems teachers can face with questioning and suggested solutions.

To get better answers from students a good starting point is to ask better questions. Question design should ensure that the questions are desirably difficult (making learners think hard and engage, without demoralising or isolating them). The questions must be accessible for all learners including students with special educational needs and disabilities (SEND) and English as additional language learners (EAL).

Chapter 2 focuses on the creation of *question banks*. They can be fantastic resources to support teacher workload, planning and preparation, consistency and learning in the classroom. The traditional technique of *hands up* is explored in Chapter 3, with several alternatives offered. *Retrieval practice*, the act of recalling information from long-term memory to enhance long-term learning, relies heavily on effective questioning; this is discussed in Chapter 4. Whether you are an experienced advocate of *multiple-choice questions*, a reluctant user or someone who never asks them, Chapter 5 contains actionable advice for every classroom. The concluding chapter encourages teachers to vary the questioning techniques they use in the classroom, with plenty of ideas and inspiration provided!

The book can be used by leaders at all levels to help colleagues with questioning in the classroom, but this *Little Guide* is aimed at classroom teachers – those that are keen to reflect on their own practice and ensure questioning is used to maximise opportunities for learning.

CHAPTER 1
QUESTIONING
'KNOW THY PURPOSE'

This chapter covers:

- **The varied reasons why teachers should ask questions**
- **Problems that can be faced with questions in the classroom**
- **Suggested solutions to the problems listed.**

WHAT IS THE PURPOSE OF QUESTIONING IN THE CLASSROOM?

Before we explore different questioning techniques, let's consider the above question. This is not a trick question. There can be several different answers. I regularly ask this question to teachers I work with as it prompts discussion, debate and reflection. Responses tend to vary, but there is consensus on the main reasons why teachers ask questions in the classroom.

Educational researcher, academic and author Professor John Hattie is widely known for his advice to teachers, which focuses on 'know thy impact' (Hattie, 2012). Awareness and evaluation of impact is an important aspect of effective questioning. However, before we consider impact it is useful to reflect on the different reasons *why* questions are asked in the classroom, the purpose. Know thy purpose.

TO ELICIT EVIDENCE OF LEARNING

This is considered the main reason for questions to be asked within a lesson. Teachers can use a range of questioning techniques to check for understanding, provide opportunities for recall, encourage elaboration and application of knowledge, vocabulary and skills. Questioning is essential to assessment, both formative and summative. Seeking evidence of learning is a particularly important motivation to ask questions, but it is not the only reason teachers should do so.

Examples of this include: quiz questions, ranging from multiple choice, short answer to extended explanations; and exam-style questions.

TO ENGAGE, EXCITE AND INSPIRE LEARNERS

Through the act of questioning, teachers can spark curiosity in the classroom, activate awe and wonder and pique interest and intrigue.

Questioning is not guaranteed to do any of the above, but it has the potential to.

Examples of this include: asking students questions about a visual image; questions to accompany a piece of text, audio or film.

TO REFLECT, SHARE AND EXPRESS

Through questioning students are provided with plentiful opportunities to reflect on their thoughts, views and knowledge. They are invited and actively encouraged to share responses with their teachers, peers and/or the whole class. Questioning is the ultimate method of amplifying student voice.

Examples of this can include: questioning techniques such as *think–pair–share* and the use of mini white boards.

TO BE INCLUSIVE

Through questioning, all learners can be involved and included in the lesson. The teacher can use a range of questioning techniques to ensure all students are able to access and understand the questions asked. If the classroom culture enables it, students should feel confident and motivated to contribute without fear or worry.

Examples of this include asking: 'What's your best answer?'; this gives students ownership and control over which response they wish to share with the teacher, peers or whole class.

TO FOCUS ATTENTION

Attention plays a crucial role in the learning process. If students are not paying attention to what they should be paying attention to, that hinders their chances of progress. The teacher can harness questioning as a method to maintain and steer student attention and focus within the lesson. Questioning can keep everyone on track, thinking about what they should be thinking about.

Examples of this include: follow-up questions, after explaining a key concept such as 'Can you explain the main differences between a sole trader and a limited company?'

TO GUIDE NEXT STEPS

Effective questioning can not only support learners, but it can also help to inform the next steps for teachers with their planning. Through the responses to questions asked, the teacher can gather data to inform what question to ask next or what direction they need to go. Questioning can reveal what learners know and what they don't know or understand yet. It is therefore crucial to closing knowledge gaps and plays a vital role with responsive and adaptive teaching. The teacher can use their professional judgement and insight to make informed decisions in terms of lesson planning.

An *exit ticket* (a question asked as the end of the lesson approaches) is a fitting example of this. The teacher can make a record of gaps in knowledge to revisit and also note content that has been fully grasped.

FOR CLASSROOM MANAGEMENT

Questioning techniques can be implemented in subtle and sophisticated ways to manage classroom behaviour and expectations. Questioning techniques can become established as classroom routines that have many benefits beyond teaching and learning.

If students know they are expected to answer questions – for example, at the start of a lesson – or they understand that the use of mini white boards means everyone must attempt to answer, then this promotes clear routines and learning behaviours.

ORACY

A wide range of key skills can be developed linked to oracy using questioning in the classroom. These include active listening, structured talk, spoken communication, choral response, pronunciation of vocabulary and more. Probing questions that go beyond single-word responses are ideal.

A geography example could be asking: 'Can you explain the different ways tourism can have a negative impact on the local area?'

CONTEXTUAL FACTORS

The factors above apply to different classroom contexts, but within those learning environments there will be additional reasons why teachers ask questions. In a science lesson, a teacher will need to check students fully understand how to safely use equipment to ensure no harm is caused. In a history lesson, a teacher can ask a question that encourages students to weigh up factors against each other, to reach a clear judgement about causes or consequences. A maths lesson will contain questions that require students to problem solve and use specific skills. In an Early Years Foundation Stage (EYFS) classroom, questioning contributes to children's speech and development, whereas at A Level a question can require students to think critically and evaluate.

An interesting activity is to ask students the following:

'Why does the teacher ask questions in a lesson?'

Their responses are likely to include the reasons above – for example, to check for learning, but they may offer alternative answers, such as 'to check we're listening' or 'to make sure we are doing what we should be'. This conversation about questioning can be used to challenge any misconceptions learners might have (arguably that the main purpose of questioning is accountability or to catch them out!).

POTENTIAL PROBLEMS AND SUGGESTED SOLUTIONS

Questioning has the potential to be immensely powerful in the classroom. However, if the questions are not carefully considered or communicated clearly then they can hinder, not help, teaching and learning. It is important when planning questions (during the curriculum design process or lesson-planning stage) to not only focus on the content and communication, but also on the purpose.

Below is a set of potential problems associated with questioning in the classroom. It can be a valuable strategy to identify problems and find applicable and relevant solutions. For each problem listed, there are solutions to help solve the issue!

Problem: Questions Asked are too Easy, or Too Difficult

If the questions asked do not provide sufficient challenge, or are too tough, then it is not a beneficial use of precious lesson time. This is where the *Goldilocks principle* applies. Questions are not too easy and obvious, not too difficult, but provide just the right amount of challenge!

Solution: Scaffolded Question Design

Closed questions tend to focus on factual recall and require short responses, but they can be challenging and make learners think hard. The teacher must also use questioning techniques that allow students to elaborate, explain and extend their responses.

Scaffolded question design allows the teacher to ask the foundational questions (not assuming students possess this level of knowledge and understanding) and then gradually increase the level of challenge. This can be done within a quiz, where the level of challenge increases with different questions, or it can be throughout a unit – as students develop their knowledge, skills, vocabulary and confidence, the questions can become more difficult.

Problem: Only Some Learners in the Class Answer Questions

This is a common problem and is often strongly associated with *hands up* questioning. When a teacher poses a question and relies on volunteers to put their hands up to answer, there are several issues with this (this is explored more fully in Chapter 3).

Solution: Use Questioning Techniques that Involve All Learners

There can be a time and place for hands up, but it should be used with caution. Questioning techniques that involve all learners should be the main method(s) used in a lesson (again, there are examples of this in Chapter 3). This could be with mini white boards, digital quizzing apps or *no hands up* questioning techniques where all students are required to be engaged and ready to respond.

Problem: Not Providing Enough Wait and Think Time for Students

A *teacher ten seconds* does not always equate to ten seconds! This is evident during questioning. Wait time does not need to be ten seconds, but it should provide the students with sufficient time to consider the question, reflect and find an answer. Asking a question and not allowing enough *wait and think* time is a problem because it can cause panic and frustration for the learner. They might not have an answer ready, whereas if they had slightly longer to prepare and think, they could respond with more depth and confidence.

Not providing enough wait and think time for students with SEND and EAL can have a negative impact, not only on their ability to generate an answer, but also on their self-esteem and confidence.

Solution: Make a Conscious Effort to Increase the Wait and Think Time

Having an awareness of the wait and think time is an important first step. The second step should be something to implement this. Hold yourself to account. Until the wait and think time becomes established as an effective classroom routine, using a stopwatch, timer or simply counting can be helpful. The challenge is to know how long the wait time should be. There is no definitive answer to this because, as with every teaching and learning approach, it depends.

Younger learners might require more time; the complexity of the question can determine how much time to provide; another factor is the student themselves and their prior knowledge. If the teacher asks a question based on curriculum content that is familiar, students are more likely to answer with greater ease and speed. The teacher should use their professional judgement to determine the wait and think time. A piece of advice I often give to teachers after lesson visits is the following: when you think you have provided enough wait time, just add slightly longer to that!

During the wait and think time it can be tempting for the teacher to provide further prompts (or even answer the questions themselves), but providing time and demonstrating patience are essential to effective classroom questioning.

Problem: Poorly Designed and Communicated Questions

If a student does not fully understand the question asked, how can they be expected to reach the correct answer? Questions can and should be challenging to make students think hard, but they should not be challenging in terms of how they are phrased and designed. Even if a student cannot answer the question, they should be able to fully understand what the question is asking. This is relevant to all learners, but once again ensuring students with SEND and EAL can access questions is vital to equitable teaching and learning.

Solution: Planning Questions Carefully

Dylan Wiliam (2014) has offered this simple, straightforward and helpful advice to teachers regarding questioning:

Plan it. Ask it. Be quiet.

This advice can appear obvious, but something I have observed with teaching (including reflecting on my own practice) is that common sense doesn't always equate to common practice. To not plan and think about the questions asked is to fail at the first hurdle! The next chapter is dedicated to *question banks*; this strategy requires teachers to carefully plan and prepare the questions they ask. The *be quiet* point links back to ensuring enough wait and think time.

Problem: The Teacher is Asking all the Questions

The teacher is the expert in the room and therefore will be guiding the lesson and the learning. However, it is important for students to understand that they can and should ask questions.

Solution: Students are Invited to Ask Questions

It is essential that teachers are asking the *right questions*, and the same applies to students. It can be frustrating when students ask endless questions without much consideration or thought, or when questions are asked that have been answered numerous times (it is important to find out if the student doesn't know because they weren't listening or they haven't grasped the concept or content yet).

Students can be provided with time and structure (in the form of sentence starters and prompts) to ask their peers questions. Time within a lesson can be dedicated to students asking their teacher questions; this could be prior to independent work or before submitting work to the teacher.

REFLECTION 1.1

Have you encountered any of the problems above in your classroom? If so, have you dealt with it or how will you deal with it?

The purpose of a question can be multifaceted. Once the purpose is carefully considered, teachers then need to focus on the question design.

NOTE THIS DOWN

What is the main purpose of questioning in your classroom?

....

....

What do your students think is the main purpose of questioning in your classroom?

....

....

Have you encountered any of the problems or challenges listed (or those not included) with questioning in the classroom?

....

....

Will you implement any of the suggested solutions in your practice?

....

....

CHAPTER 2
QUESTION BANKS FOR TEACHING AND LEARNING

This chapter covers:

- The concept of question banks
- The benefits of using question banks
- Advice and guidance about question bank creation
- Examples of how question banks can be used to enhance teaching and learning.

WHAT ARE QUESTION BANKS?

Question banks are a collection of questions that teachers are required to ask and students are required to answer. Question banks bring the curriculum to life as the questions draw on the curriculum content. The questions within the question bank(s) should cover everything students are expected to know and do. This includes focusing on key vocabulary and definitions, key facts, concepts, significant dates and individuals, translations, quotations and features.

The answers should be clearly included alongside the questions. This can be challenging for extended essay-style questions or discussion starters, but general points can be included in the answer section or links to mark schemes.

There is no set rule as to how many questions should be included within a question bank, or how it should be created and laid out. All these decisions can be made by the teacher(s) using their professional judgement and expertise. Question banks tend to be divided up into units and topics (or subtopics). They are not set in stone, but instead living documents that can be reviewed and, if needed, adapted and improved.

WHAT ARE THE BENEFITS OF USING QUESTION BANKS?

I am an advocate for the creation and use of question banks because of the many benefits they offer teachers, leaders, students and parents. Below is a summary of ten benefits of using them (in no particular order).

1   *Consistency*: Teachers across a department and phase are asking learners the same questions. There is flexibility for adaptive teaching, but this guarantees the core curriculum content is covered.

2. *Professional autonomy*: Teachers can use the questions from the question banks in the way they wish. For example, one teacher might use a digital quiz, whereas another teacher might prefer to ask the same questions using mini white boards. Question banks enable the right balance between consistency and context.
3. *Quality assurance*: Question banks allow leaders at all levels to ensure the questions asked are linked to the curriculum and contain the appropriate level of support and challenge.
4. *Sustainable workload*: If created collaboratively or via the use of technology (see later in this chapter for more information about digital creation), this can save a significant amount of teacher time.
5. *Support for early career teachers* (ECTs): Teachers early in their career can lack experience and confidence with question design and delivery, therefore having access to question banks can be a supportive and useful teaching and learning aid.
6. *Support for non-specialist teachers*: As more teachers are expected to teach outside their subject or phase specialism, question banks can be a helpful resource to ensure the correct questions are being asked.
7. *Can be used to support staff absence*: Staff absence is not ideal, but this is the reality that every school will encounter at some point. Schools should be ready to support absent staff and staff that will be teaching their classes, from cover supervisors to supply teachers.
8. *Question banks can be shared with students*: There are numerous ways students can use question banks. Within a lesson students can use the resource for self- and/or pair quizzing and self-/peer assessment. Outside a lesson they can use question banks to prepare for assessment, assist with home learning and with the creation of study materials such as *flashcards*.

9. *Question banks can be shared with parents*: Parents may wish to help their child with their learning and independent study, but they could lack the knowledge, skills, or confidence to do so. Question banks can be shared so that questions can be asked outside the lesson. The answer sheet can enable parents to provide immediate feedback to their child.
10. *Used by external visitors*: When an external observer (ranging from a senior leader to inspector) visits a lesson, they cannot simply ask students random questions. They need to ensure the questions asked are relevant and link back to the curriculum. If observers are equipped with a series of questions and answers, this can be used to encourage meaningful dialogue between the visitor and students.

HOW TO CREATE A QUESTION BANK

There are several ways to create question banks. There is no 'one size fits all' approach. The decision on how to create one can be determined by the number of staff within a department or phase, the levels of experience and expertise, workload considerations and the context of the learners.

Using Generative Artificial Intelligence (Gen AI)

AI is a hot topic in education and isn't going anywhere! Harnessing the benefits of AI can help teachers in numerous ways. In terms of question banks, Gen AI tools (such as Microsoft Co-Pilot™, Google Gemini™, or ChatGPT™) can generate a bank of relevant questions for teachers. The teacher will need to input information about the questions; the more data included the better the generated content will be.

For example, instead of requesting a question bank for GCSE English Literature it would be better to add more specific details including the exam specification and the unit/topic. Question banks can be generated at a rapid pace and further prompts (suggestions/requests) can be entered to add, amend or remove any questions – all of which takes a fraction of the amount of time it would take a teacher to think up or copy from textbook materials. Teacher input is still present for quality assurance.

Gen AI can create question banks with a range of different question formats, including multiple choice, short answer, discussion prompts, matching and fill in the blanks tasks, plus more. The question banks can be saved as a Word™ doc or PDF, so paper copies can be used. Alternatively, digital question banks can be transferred to a virtual learning environment (VLE) such as the Google Classroom™.

It is possible for teachers to create question banks without the support of Gen AI, but, as mentioned, this could take more time, effort, and energy. There are pre-made question banks available online, but it is important to carefully check if they are relevant and age-appropriate. There are online quizzing platforms that provide teachers and students with pre-made question banks. The collections of questions can cover a specific unit or can be broken down into subtopics; they can be suitable for a specific curriculum or examination board. Examples include Quizlet™, Quizizz™, Carousel Learn™ and EduCake™.

When collating questions from any online source (including Gen AI) the teacher should check for accuracy, as errors can be made with spellings, phrasing and the answers provided! In addition to mistakes, Gen AI could produce content that is not age-appropriate, is of mediocre quality or irrelevant.

In June 2025, the Department for Education (DfE) published guidance for schools about the use of AI in education. The guidance stated the following:

'Generative AI tools can make certain written tasks quicker and easier, but … cannot replace the judgement and deep subject knowledge of a human expert.'

I believe that is an essential message, worth echoing.

CASE STUDY

Question Banks Across a Secondary Department

Within a secondary department of four members of staff, the Head of Department decides to introduce question banks to support teacher workload and departmental consistency. They make the decision to implement the question banks at Key Stage 3 to begin with a focus on the curriculum content taught in the first academic term. Staff are instructed to do this in advance, so they have what is agreed to be enough time.

Three members of the department (this includes the Head of Department and two experienced teachers) are each given a year group to lead with. The fourth member of the department is an ECT. They have been assigned to support one of the experienced teachers, so they can observe the process of question bank creation and design, with the aim of developing them independently in the future.

The teachers can use resources available to them (online materials, textbooks and knowledge organisers) and have the option to use Gen AI, if they wish. There is a soft deadline set; after that date, staff will use designated departmental time after school to review, discuss and quality assure the question banks. The workload has been shared fairly, but they will come together collaboratively to check and provide feedback.

Once created, the question banks are stored on a shared file that all staff can access. The teachers will trial the use of question banks, with a planned reflection meeting scheduled later in the term. If the department agrees they are a helpful resource, further plans will be made to create more question banks for other units and year groups.

> Teachers can then use them alongside a range of questioning techniques in the classroom. The organisation of question banks is important to ensure they can be widely and extensively used. Securing them in relevant and organised folders is the simplest way to store them.

If working in a primary context, it can be useful for all teachers to have access to question banks across the school. The Year 6 teacher, teaching the topic of plants in science, can access questions from the Year 4 question banks on plants to revisit and retrieve information from previously taught content. In a secondary context, it can be useful for different subjects to have access to question banks, especially where there are cross-curricular links. The Year 9 English teacher can select and copy relevant World War I questions from the history department Year 9 question bank, as students are learning about World War I poetry and there is curriculum content overlap.

# NOTE THIS DOWN

Do you use question banks? If so, what are the benefits you have found? If not, how do you plan to use question banks?

....

....

How do you or will you share question banks with students and parents?

....

....

Who could you collaborate with to create and quality assure question banks? This could include school or multi-academy trust (MAT) colleagues, professional learning communities, online networks or another group.

....

....

CHAPTER 3
ALTERNATIVES TO 'HANDS UP'

This chapter covers:

- The problems with 'hands up' in the classroom
- Techniques to involve and engage all learners
- When to use 'hands up' in the classroom.

THE 'HANDS UP' APPROACH

The teacher poses a question; a smattering of hands shoot up into the air. The teacher selects a student to respond and the teacher replies with feedback. There are variations of this, but it's an accurate description of a common occurrence in the classroom. I used to teach this way and I still find myself sometimes reverting to hands up; it can be a hard habit for the teacher to kick!

Opting for a hands up approach feels natural, for the teacher and student. It enables students that want to contribute or know the answer to participate in the class discussion. The teacher doesn't feel like they are picking on students, making anyone feel uncomfortable or anxious and they are also providing the students that want it with the opportunity to be involved. Hands up ensures no one shouts out or interrupts someone else. Great, so what's the problem? Well, there are several issues with hands up …

WHAT ARE THE PROBLEMS WITH HANDS UP TO ANSWER QUESTIONS IN THE CLASSROOM?

When hands up is the dominant questioning technique, it tends to be the same students answering questions every lesson (and therefore the same students avoiding answering questions every lesson). The answers provided by a small sample of students can be very misleading for the teacher. It is not an accurate reflection of the whole class, just a snapshot of a select few.

This is not an inclusive approach. If learners aren't encouraged to engage, they can coast in a lesson, lose focus and struggle with attention. Their voices are not being heard, and they are not contributing to the lesson. Inclusivity involves using a range of strategies and techniques so all learners can flourish. There are often varied reasons why students are reluctant (or even refuse) to participate in class discussions. Awareness of the issue is important for the teacher, so they can then use the relevant and appropriate interventions, as shown in the examples below.

Example 1: A Student with Dyslexia

A student with dyslexia could be worried about reading answers aloud in class, therefore this threat can be removed. Students can be provided with text in advance to read and become familiar with (including seeking clarification or explanation from the teacher). Alternatively, the teacher can ask the student a question that does not rely on reading information from their class book or the board, but instead allows them to share their thoughts, opinions or views linked to the curriculum content.

Example 2: An EAL Learner

During a class question and answer session an EAL learner could become nervous about verbally responding in front of the class, as they fear they might not use the correct terminology, or their pronunciation could be wrong. Creating a classroom culture where learners can make mistakes without repercussions such as humiliation is crucial. The teacher can use a range of techniques to support EAL students, including the use of mini white boards, matching tasks, closed questions, agree or disagree and the use of non-verbal gestures such as thumbs up or down, fingers on chin to show thinking or finger digits in the air to represent an action or answer.

Example 3: Struggling with Maths

In a maths lesson, there is a student that believes they can't do maths and thinks they are bad at the subject. In other lessons, they are keen to answer questions and get involved, just not in maths. The teacher realises the student mindset and motivation is the issue. The teacher has tried to scaffold questions, asking the individual easier questions to build their confidence in the subject. Unfortunately, this well-intentioned technique (which could work with some students) backfired as the student was aware they were being asked the 'easier' questions compared to their peers, adding to their insecurities in maths.

The teacher is unsure what to do as this is a subject-specific issue; asking other teachers of this student is unlikely to be helpful. The teacher decides to talk to a maths colleague, as they taught this student maths last academic year.

During this conversation the former maths teacher of the student recognises this issue with this individual; thanks to their experience, they can offer helpful advice. The suggestion provided is to use precise praise, where relevant and appropriate. Last year, the teacher noticed this individual responded well to precise praise and was gradually becoming more confident within the subject. Praise can be written or verbal, but it should be authentic and genuine. This was something the teacher tried in the following lesson. The praise was specific and highlighted a key strength with strategic thinking and completing the process correctly. Questions targeted at this individual were linked to the precise praise, but kept the level of challenge; the student responded with greater ease and confidence. There is still much to be done to build the self-esteem of the student and improve their attitude towards the subject, but it was a positive first step in the right direction.

GIVE STUDENTS THE 'GREEN LIGHT'

For the students that struggle to answer questions in front of their peers or contribute to classroom discussions, this technique is designed to build their level of confidence and gain experience responding in class. During the lesson, when students are on task or perhaps when they are talking in pairs as part of *turn and talk* or *think–pair–share*, the teacher can have a conversation with the learner, one to one, about their answers. This is a private conversation between the teacher and learner, therefore the stakes can feel lower than contributing to a whole-class discussion.

During this conversation, the teacher will give feedback to the student. This feedback can inform the student if they are correct or not with precise praise awarded. Later, when the teacher brings the class together to consolidate, check for understanding or ask broad questions, they can include the student to whom they have already spoken. They can ask the reluctant student to share with the rest of the class, for example: 'Hazel, please can you tell the class what you answered for question five?'

The student was told earlier in the lesson that their answer to question five was correct, so this removes the risk of making a mistake publicly. By confirming their answer was correct the teacher has given them the green light; the purpose of this is to create opportunities to include learners, develop their oracy skills and build confidence in the classroom.

Now, let's look at some specific alternative techniques to hands up in the classroom.

COLD CALLING

This questioning technique is attributed to Doug Lemov, author of *Teach Like a Champion 3.0* (2021). There is more to *cold calling* than no hands up (although that can often be the perception). The purpose of this questioning technique is to encourage all learners to think about the question posed, provide all learners with wait and think time and then the teacher will decide which student to select to respond.

If implemented correctly it can be a game changer in the classroom. However, it can be difficult for the teacher to get right. I struggled with this technique in my classroom, but through combining reflection and resilience I was able to effectively embed cold calling as a classroom routine. Below are some practical tips for using it in the classroom.

1. *Always use student names*: this helps to keep the questioning warm, friendly and low stakes. It is not about catching students out or making anyone uncomfortable (obviously, that is never desirable in the classroom). When meeting new classes, seating plans combined with cold calling can help the teacher learn new names. At the start of the academic year, I ask my classes to wear sticky labels with their names written clearly, to use during questioning, feedback conversations and to help me learn their names.

2. *Allow hands up*: this might sound contradictory, but allowing hands up still enables the teacher to select the student that responds. The teacher can pick a student with or without their hand up. Allowing hands up shows the teacher which students believe they know the answer (although it doesn't guarantee it's the correct answer!) and shows which students want to contribute.

3. *Observe others cold calling*: I have had the privilege to observe many lessons. Through this I have witnessed excellent examples of this technique implemented effectively in the classroom. Observe colleagues or find videos to view online. Observation and reflection are a powerful combination.

4. *Ask for feedback*: invite colleagues to informally visit your lesson and observe your questioning. Talk to students, ask how they feel about this approach and your questioning techniques. Do your students understand what cold calling is and why it is used in the classroom? Find out or double check to be sure. They could have misconceptions about this technique, again with more of a focus on accountability rather than learning.

5. *Combine cold calling with other questioning techniques*: I found this the best method to help me effectively use cold calling in the classroom. I combined this technique with think–pair–share. This combination ensured everyone had individual think time, followed by an opportunity to discuss their answer with a peer;

cold calling could be used for the final stage, by which time all students should have something to share with the class. The green light technique also works well with cold calling.

Another powerful questioning technique that can be used as an alternative to hands up is the use of mini white boards. This is explored in the last chapter, with practical examples and tips.

RANDOM NAME GENERATORS

There are mixed feelings about the use of *random name generators* in the classroom. As with any classroom technique there can be pros and cons or pay-offs and trade-offs! A random name generator can be a digital tool (a great example of this is www.classtools.net/random-name-picker/) or it can involve names on a lollypop stick, or picked out of a hat!

The teacher should ask the question prior to selecting a student at random to answer; if the student is selected prior to the question the rest of the class can switch off and not even attempt to consider a response. Selecting a digital tool that takes a few seconds to spin or select a name can help the teacher to ensure they are providing the thinking time, as the wait time is built in as part of the process! This message was echoed in a meta-analysis published in 2025 by Yu et al. (p. 31).The authors provided the following advice:

> 'Randomly calling a student to answer a question and leaving all other students silently listening is not a good choice. A better practice is to require all students to overtly answer practice questions.'

Overt retrieval requires students to generate an answer from long-term memory. This contrasts with *covert* retrieval practice, which involves learners mentally recalling information from long-term memory, but they are not required to share that information through a written or verbal response. The meta-analysis concluded that thinking about a response (covert retrieval) did produce a benefit in learning. Yu et al. (2025, p. 31) state:

> *'The results showed that covert retrieval enhances learning to a small but significant extent, and its effectiveness is moderated by several factors including provision of corrective feedback, control strategy, and retention interval.'*

This has important implications when considering and communicating questions. If students are rehearsing an answer and thinking about information internally this can help their learning. The challenge for teachers is: how do we know what our students are thinking? Unless they share that information (through overt retrieval practice), there is no way to know for sure, hence the need for a variety of questioning techniques. Overt retrieval practice will lead to greater learning benefits and gains, through the act of retrieving information or an answer.

The main argument for using random name generators is to remove any unconscious teacher bias, thus ensuring someone is picked at random instead of the same reliable students being called upon by the teacher. It can promote fairness and balance. This technique can be fun and engaging for learners (although, if it fills some students with dread then it will need to be introduced once students are used to answering questions in class or not used at all). All learners need to be prepared and ready, as they could be randomly selected, therefore this can support focus and attention.

The argument against random name generators is that it can limit the teacher. The teacher doesn't know which student will be selected, so they don't know if the level of challenge is appropriate or not. I would recommend using the random name generator with questions that are designed to consolidate or retrieve knowledge. Therefore, the questions asked are questions that students have been asked before and are more likely to be successful. Another method is to allow the random student selected to 'phone a friend' and to confer with their partner briefly.

CHORAL RESPONSE

This technique requires everyone in the class to answer a question verbally (in contrast to targeting individuals) or recite a term, quote, or poem in unison. This technique is not limited to questioning, as the teacher can ask the class to repeat after them. This can be used to practise the pronunciation of key vocabulary, to support language learning and offer opportunities for rehearsal and repetition.

Peps McCrea, Director of Education at StepLab, (2024) writes the following about *choral response*:

> 'When we embed choral response in our practice, not only do we help consolidate ideas and create the conditions for better elaboration, but it also enables us to: bolster our checking for understanding, boost student motivation through quick wins, build feelings of belonging through shared rituals, and reduce attentional drift. And (as per pretty much all effective teaching), it tends to benefit those with special needs the most.'

Choral response can be used across a range of subjects and with different ages. It is a misconception to think this technique is only suitable for younger learners or language learning. Examples of choral response include:

- *maths*: answering quick-fire multiplication questions;
- *history*: the teacher states a key historical event; students respond on 1–2–3 with the correct date;
- *English literature*: a teacher begins a quote from Macbeth; the class completes the quote together;
- *PE*: before playing badminton, the teacher stands in various positions and the class must respond together, naming the position 'serve';
- *science*: a diagram of the breathing system is presented on the board for the class to see; there are no labels or text. When the teacher points to a specific section of the diagram the class must collectively name the part of the diagram – for example, 'alveoli'.

Naturally, choral response lends itself to short-answer questions. Questions that require explanation, or where a variety of responses would be accurate, are not appropriate.

 **CASE STUDY**

Observing Common Questioning Challenges

A Year 1 teacher has been observed by her line manager. The Year 1 teacher anticipated what the feedback would be: to develop questioning in the classroom. The teacher was asking a variety of questions, pitched to the right level and communicated clearly, but there were several issues with the questioning technique.

The first issue was the hands up approach. Half of the class were enthusiastic and keen to engage, but others showed no interest. The second issue was linked to questioning and classroom management, as some students were shouting out responses without being instructed to do so.

The observer explained how these are common problems in the classroom, but there are ways to overcome them. The starting point should be to explain to the class (in a student-friendly way) why everyone is expected to contribute to the lesson and why every voice in the classroom matters. Following on from this, a link can be made to behaviour policy regarding shouting out, regularly reminding students about classroom expectations.

It was then suggested that the teacher selects a technique to trial that involves all learners responding and answering questions. The teacher decided to implement choral response as the action point moving forward, alongside clear conversations with students about learning and behaviour. The observer also invited the Year 1 teacher to visit their classroom, with a focus on observing questioning techniques in action.

WHEN TO USE HANDS UP IN A LESSON

Author Tom Sherrington has written about the pitfalls of hands up, but he is aware there can be a time and place for hands to go in the air! Sherrington (2022) writes:

> *'There are some very important uses of hands up; it's helpful to have good routines around each one so that you are inviting hands up in a deliberate way for a specific purpose, not simply allowing it to become the casually lazy default and thus allowing some students to dominate and others to become passive.'*

Sherrington suggests that there are times in the class where hands up can be used appropriately, to support behaviour and learning in the lesson; they are:

1. *hands up to confirm*: the teacher could ask for a quick show of hands from the class to confirm they are equipped and ready for the lesson, or to gauge a class response to a question such as, 'Hands up if you have been to the local history museum?';
2. *hands up for ideas*: this is to enable students to add something else to a response or to the class discussion. This allows learners to develop or build on an original answer and elaborate further;
3. *hands up for questions*: as mentioned, students asking questions in class is something to encourage. The questions can vary from asking to go to the toilet to asking for support or asking a question linked to the curriculum content, but whatever the question is, hands up ensures no shouting out or disruption;

4 *hands up to volunteer:* if the teacher has asked a particularly challenging question, it could be appropriate for the teacher to ask for hands up if anyone wishes to volunteer to answer.

This chapter is not about condemning the use of hands up in the classroom, but instead raising awareness of the likely problems – and providing some suggested solutions.

NOTE THIS DOWN

When do you use hands up in the classroom?

....

....

How do you ensure all learners are engaged and included when asking questions in a lesson?

....

....

What alternatives to hands up questioning do you use in the classroom?

....

....

What is your main practical takeaway from this chapter?

....

....

CHAPTER 4
RETRIEVAL PRACTICE

This chapter covers:

- What retrieval practice is (and what it isn't)
- The reasons why teachers, students and parents should embrace retrieval practice
- When to provide opportunities for retrieval practice
- Cued recall in the classroom
- Free recall in the classroom.

WHAT IS RETRIEVAL PRACTICE?

Most teachers are likely to be familiar with the term and concept of *retrieval practice*. It is the act of recalling previously taught content/information from long-term memory, to enhance long-term learning.

Every time an individual uses their long-term memory they improve their long-term memory. Information becomes easier and quicker to retrieve in the future because of retrieval practice (although retrieval strength, the ability to retrieve information, can and does fluctuate).

Revisiting prior learning via *reminders* is different from retrieval practice. Reminders can include showing a video to the class to recap content or presenting previous slides, worksheets, or a knowledge organiser to review and discuss. There can be benefits to providing reminders, especially if an extended period of time has passed since the content was covered, but the purpose and nature of the task is not retrieval practice.

I have observed tasks where students can find and copy the correct answers, either through searching in their class notes or using information from classroom displays. Again, this is not retrieval practice, as they are not generating the answer from long-term memory. Retrieval practice should be closed book (with information on displays hidden or removed). If students do take an open book approach, because they were absent in a previous lesson or do not know/cannot retrieve the correct answer, they should write any information/response in a different colour to illustrate that the answer was copied, not retrieved (this is useful for the learner and teacher).

Retrieval practice can be implemented using a range of formats including multiple-choice questions, using cues and prompts, verbal retrieval tasks, demonstrations, flashcards and examination-style questions. It should be low stakes; this helps (although does not guarantee) to avoid stress, pressure and anxiety in lessons. Feedback should always be provided. Retrieval practice opportunities can occur inside and outside the classroom. In addition to being an evidence-informed strategy, it can be engaging, enjoyable and rewarding for learners.

THE BENEFITS OF RETRIEVAL PRACTICE

In a meta-analysis of ten learning techniques, authored by Gregory Donoghue and John Hattie (2021), retrieval practice was found to be one of the two techniques with the highest utility (alongside *spaced practice*, which refers to distributed practice in contrast to cramming). Based on this conclusion, the authors recommended that educators, students and parents embrace retrieval practice as it can be a powerful learning strategy.

The positive effect retrieval practice can have on student learning and progress is enough to justify its place in the classroom, but there are other benefits linked to embracing it. The indirect benefits include the following:

- retrieval practice can have a high impact on student overall confidence and wellbeing (Agarwal et al., 2014);
- if used at the start of a lesson, teachers have reported retrieval practice tasks help to settle the class and have a positive impact on classroom behaviour (Bates and Shea, 2024);
- low-stakes quizzes can be easy and cheap to implement (Perry et al., 2021);
- quizzing can reveal misconceptions and identify gaps in knowledge (Perry et al., 2021);
- retrieval practice can lead to better organisation of knowledge, improvement in the transfer of knowledge to new concepts and can provide useful feedback and insight for teachers (Roediger et al., 2011).

It is important to note that the benefits listed are not guaranteed and depend on a range of variables, but they are useful to be aware of and strive for.

REFLECTION 4.1

What benefits have you noticed from providing retrieval practice opportunities in the classroom?

WHEN SHOULD OPPORTUNITIES FOR RETRIEVAL PRACTICE BE PROVIDED?

This question is often discussed amongst teachers and has led to the belief that retrieval practice must be at the start of a lesson. There are several arguments to suggest this is a suitable time within a lesson to provide opportunities for retrieval. This does not mean retrieval practice should become limited to these first five minutes. In terms of when to use retrieval practice, remember the Nike™ campaign: *Just Do It*. Questioning that requires students to retrieve an answer from long-term memory can be carried out at any point in the lesson, and should be encouraged outside the classroom too (as homework or independent study).

Curriculum design and planning should factor in the role of regular retrieval practice. When teachers race through curriculum content and fail to include plenty of opportunities for retrieval practice, it is likely students will struggle to retrieve the information when they need it.

Students also need to understand the importance of embracing retrieval practice and spaced practice. If students study the night before an exam or assessment with retrieval practice, this cramming will not be as beneficial as shorter bursts, little and often, with spaced practice. In the past I have argued the sooner, the better with retrieval practice … but there is a caveat to this. Retrieval strength, as mentioned earlier in this chapter, fluctuates; therefore once students can retrieve information quickly, confidently and correctly the challenge becomes to maintain this level of retrieval strength. The student could tick something off their revision list and assume that is the end of that, but the reality is they could struggle to retrieve the information when needed if they have not retrieved it for a prolonged period of time. Slow and steady wins the retrieval race!

CUED RECALL

This is an example of retrieval practice where a *cue* or prompt is provided for learners. The cues can include visual images, audio clips, key words, or verbal prompts from the teacher. It is important the cue does not provide too much support for the learner, as this will dilute the effectiveness of retrieval practice. This is known in cognitive psychology as the *cue overload principle*.

Cued recall can support learners to achieve retrieval success. All learners can benefit from the use of cued recall, with the aim to remove the cues like a form of scaffolding in the classroom. Research (Karpicke et al., 2016) has suggested that younger learners need more explicit guidance and cues for the initial retrieval task. Students with SEND and EAL learners can also benefit from cued recall.

DESCRIBE IT, RETRIEVE IT; *CUED RECALL TASK*

This task involves presenting a visual image to the class. Ideally, it should be an image students have already seen, as the *encoding specificity principle* (Tulving and Thomson, 1973) suggests that retrieval cues will be more useful if they were presented in the encoding stages (where new information is introduced). Students are tasked to describe what is happening in the picture. All students should be able to do this – even if they were absent previously, they can still describe what they can see. Students can do this through a verbal or written response. The second part of the task requires students to retrieve additional information from long-term memory, linked to the image. The picture will trigger their memory, with the aim to take them back to the encoding lesson so they can retrieve relevant information.

CUE CARDS

The teacher can instruct learners to find and use cues if they are struggling to retrieve information from long-term memory. The cues could be in the format of flashcards with key terms, definitions, images, or hints. The *cue cards* could provide sentence starters or show students how to solve a problem/answer the question, without revealing any answers! It is important that the cue cards don't contain detailed information or answers for copying and transfer. They should be designed to be helpful yet still ensure students think hard and retrieve information from long-term memory.

The cue cards could be presented as a hint sheet, knowledge organiser, bookmark, or a visible display in the classroom. The teacher or Gen AI can create them.

Teachers can add more cues to increase the level of support provided, or they can remove cues to increase the level of challenge. It is for the teacher to use their professional judgement and knowledge of the content and individual learner to inform their decision.

FREE RECALL

Professor Robert Bjork, a world-leading expert in the field of memory, stated (in Jones, 2021, p. 61):

> 'The more involved or difficult the act of retrieval – provided it succeeds – the larger the benefits in terms of recall.'

Free recall is the most challenging form of retrieval practice. Free recall tasks can provide opportunities for verbal or written responses. The questions can require short answers or an extended essay.

It is important to think about the question asked for any free recall task. The two questions below are both examples of free recall, but there is a key difference.

- *Q1. What can you recall about Vincent Van Gogh?*
- *Q2. What can you recall about the artwork by Vincent Van Gogh?*

The first question is more open; students could include details about the life, character and legacy of Vincent Van Gogh, in addition to information about his artwork. The second question is specifically focused on asking students to retrieve information about artwork by Van Gogh. The second is an example of *guided* free recall, where the question guides the retrieval and therefore answers are more likely to be relevant and focused.

There can be a place for guided and open free recall in the classroom, but when students don't include information in their answers that the teacher hoped or expected them to, it is not the fault of the learner. The only way students will know what we want them to retrieve is to communicate that clearly through the question design. Better questions often lead to better answers.

Gen AI can create a range of free recall tasks to provide learners with a variety of retrieval practice opportunities. It is not only teachers that can use Gen AI to support question and task design; a study published in 2025 by Monzon and Hays, stated the following (on p. 1):

> 'For learners, Gen AI offers unprecedented self-directed learning opportunities, improved cognitive engagement, and effective retrieval practices, leading to enhanced autonomy, motivation, and knowledge retention.'

Although there are concerns about how students will use AI (with child safety online and plagiarism), there are ways students can use Gen AI to support their studies. With Gen AI students can generate questions, quizzes and past examination-style questions to answer and seek feedback on. It can be helpful to share useful prompts and guidance with learners about the use of Gen AI to ensure they are accessing correct and relevant information and support.

The effectiveness of retrieval practice as a strategy, to support teaching and learning, is widely cited in academic literature and has been echoed by enthusiastic teachers that have embraced it in their classrooms. The effectiveness is determined by a range of variables. Questioning, from design to delivery, is a crucial component of effectively embedding retrieval practice inside and outside the classroom.

NOTE THIS DOWN

What does retrieval practice look like in your classroom?

....

....

When do you typically provide opportunities for retrieval practice in the classroom?

....

....

Have you encountered any obstacles with implementing retrieval practice in the classroom?

....

....

How do you encourage/support learners to use retrieval practice as a learning strategy outside the classroom?

....

....

What are your three key takeaways from this chapter?

....

....

CHAPTER 5
MULTIPLE-CHOICE QUESTIONS

This chapter covers:

- Guidance about multiple-choice question design
- Different approaches to multiple-choice question creation
- Different approaches to multiple-choice questions and quizzes
- Multiple-choice questions and the best feedback techniques to use.

MULTIPLE-CHOICE QUESTIONS IN THE CLASSROOM

Multiple-choice questions are useful for checking for understanding, consolidating knowledge and, as discussed in the previous chapter, providing opportunities for retrieval practice. They can be used at different points in the learning process; this is a benefit because the same multiple-choice quiz or questions can (and should) be asked more than once. Multiple-choice questions can be designed to tackle misconceptions and make students think hard.

As with any questioning technique, multiple-choice questions have their limitations. They should not be used as the sole method of questioning – rather in combination with other questioning techniques. Too much reliance on multiple-choice questions can limit the opportunities students have to recall information as they don't allow for elaboration and in-depth explanations.

The right time to use them should be determined by the purpose (as discussed in Chapter 1). They can be used at the end of a lesson on an 'exit ticket' to check for understanding, or used at the start of a lesson to provide an opportunity to ask questions based on prior learning.

It is worth noting that multiple-choice questions provide students with the correct answer to select. Therefore, this is regarded as recognition or cued recall, in contrast to free recall where learners must generate the answer from long-term memory. I have tended to use multiple-choice questions when I want to ask a lot of questions in a short amount of time, as it is possible to do so this way. Multiple-choice questions can be used to build confidence and provide initial retrieval success, but there must be a point where questioning extends beyond multiple-choice questions.

MULTIPLE-CHOICE QUESTION DESIGN

Naturally, the starting point will be the question. If there are question banks available (as discussed in Chapter 2), the questions can be converted into multiple-choice questions. Ideally, the question should be one that can be used when the multiple-choice options are removed, as shown with the example below.

Q. What is the name of Juliet's cousin?

a   Mercutio

b   Benvolio

c   Tybalt

The same question can be asked again, in a different lesson and using a different technique.

Q. What is the name of Juliet's cousin?

Answer: Tybalt

For example, it could be used with cold calling, choral response or answers on a mini white board.

The language and phrasing of the question must be accessible for all. It is important that multiple-choice questions are challenging (students are already presented with the correct response so there is a level of support provided), but the question should be easy to understand. If there are challenging terms, it would be better to check for understanding prior to including them in the question quiz. The example below is asking students to select the correct historical date, but they can only do so if they know and understand what the term 'conscription' means.

Q. What year was conscription introduced?

a   1914

b   1916

c   1918

I believe the secret ingredient to a successful multiple-choice question is not the question (although that is especially important!), but instead the plausible distractors that are included. The other two options (I advise a total of three options to manage cognitive load) should have a link to the question. They should not be completely random, funny, or just there as a filler, as this decreases the level of challenge and therefore the overall level of effectiveness. The previous example, asking about the date conscription was introduced, contains three key dates. Each date is relevant to the topic of World War I and therefore requires students to think and select carefully.

Multiple-choice questions can help students to select the correct answer to show they know it, where they might otherwise struggle in writing the answer down (if they find spellings of key terms and answers difficult). This is illustrated in the example below.

Q. Which of the following is the term used to describe the belief in one God?

a Atheism

b Monotheism

c Polytheism

This provides further exposure to tier 3 terminology and can show if students recognise the accurate term; next steps can focus on retrieving the correct definition from memory and spelling the key term accurately.

MULTIPLE-CHOICE QUESTION CREATION

Once again, teachers can use digital platforms and Gen AI to create multiple-choice questions. They can search online quizzing tools for pre-made multiple-choice quizzes and decide if they are relevant/appropriate to use (some quiz platforms allow users to take questions from other quizzes and adapt them for their classroom context – for example, this is known as the 'Teleport Feature' on Quizizz). Teachers can provide an instruction to Gen AI, with guidance about the content, age group and level of challenge, in addition to how many questions to include and how to format them.

If creating multiple-choice questions from scratch, this can be time-consuming and, at times, a challenge for the teacher to generate plausible distractors. Gen AI can create a multiple-choice quiz at rapid speed. It can adjust the questions, based on the prompts it receives. For example, through uploading an existing list of questions or a resource such as a knowledge organiser, Gen AI can create a ten-question multiple-choice quiz based on the uploaded content. Once the multiple-choice questions have been created the teacher can choose to adapt them further or download ready for use.

DIFFERENT APPROACHES TO MULTIPLE-CHOICE QUESTIONS

Multiple-choice questions can be presented to students digitally, via online quizzing tools, but students will require devices to access; not all schools have (or allow) access to individual devices within lessons. Gen AI multiple-choice questions can be downloaded and printed for paper quizzes or copied and pasted into slide show presentations to present to the class.

Students can use mini white boards to write their response to the multiple-choice questions. This is an ideal use of mini white boards because the teacher can immediately view all the responses with ease, provide immediate feedback and respond to any misconceptions or queries.

EXTENDING MULTIPLE-CHOICE QUESTIONS

There are numerous ways multiple-choice questions can be adapted to gauge more information from learners.

Confidence Ratings

After each multiple-choice question, students can be asked to self-assess their levels of *confidence*. This can be using numbers, as shown with the example below. Alternatively, students can select words from

'Very confident' to 'Not very' and other phrases in between. Students could simply circle an emoji/smiley face which best reflects their level of confidence.

> *Q. Which of the following key terms refers to how high or low a note is?*
>
> a Tempo
>
> b Pitch
>
> c Motif
>
> Confidence rating scale (1 = Not confident, 10 = Very confident). Circle the number that best represents how confident you are about your answer. List the numbers after the rating scale.

This can be insightful for the teacher and students. Through using confidence ratings teachers can learn what questions students lacked confidence with, or which questions attracted the most guesses as responses. For the students, the confidence rating can be insightful as it helps them to develop a better awareness of what they know and don't know yet. Students can be surprised when they selected a confident rating, only to learn later they were wrong! Alternatively, students can be pleasantly surprised when they lack confidence, but their answer was accurate.

Elaborate and Extend

This technique (Jones, 2022) encourages students to add additional information if they have completed the multiple-choice question quiz, as shown with the PE example in Table 5.1.

Other ways this technique can be used include asking students to show workings out, instructing learners to explain why the other options are incorrect or simply as an opportunity for them to share something else they know that is linked to the question.

Table 5.1 An example of the elaborate and extend technique

Multiple-choice question	Elaboration
Read the question carefully and highlight what you think is the correct answer	Do you know anything else you can add that is linked to this question? Any further information can be included in the column

1 Which one of these components of fitness is measured by the ruler drop test?
  a Balance
  b Coordination
  c Reaction time
	The aim of the ruler drop test is to find out how fast someone's reaction time is. The test finds out how long it takes someone to react to the dropped ruler by measuring how far it falls before being caught

Audio Multiple-Choice Questions

There are different variations of this. One example is where students listen to the teacher (or a digital recording) read the questions and options. This can be combined with mini white boards or paper quizzing. The example below involves a Welsh second-language teacher reading the question and statements aloud to the class.

Q. Which of the following is the correct translation of 'I like history because it is interesting'?

a Dwi'n hoffi hanes achos mae'n diddorol

b Dwi'n hoffi gwyddoniaeth achos mae'n diddorol

c Dwi'n casau hanes achos mae'n ddiflas

The students listen carefully and note down a, b or c based on what they think is the correct answer (a). The teacher can repeat the question and statements if necessary. This approach to multiple-choice questions provides an opportunity for students to practice listening, an important skill.

The same question could be presented to students visually as text, in a previous or following lesson. To extend the multiple-choice question further, students could be tasked to translate the incorrect options, as shown in Table 5.2.

Table 5.2 Visual representation of an audio multiple-choice question

Highlight the correct answer	Translate the incorrect options
a Dwi'n hoffi hanes achos mae'n diddorol	
b Dwi'n hoffi gwyddoniaeth achos mae'n diddorol	b I like science because it's interesting
c Dwi'n casau hanes achos mae'n ddiflas	c I hate history because it's boring

Another way to extend this would be to ask students if they agree with the correct statement and to explain their reasons. If asking questions using vocabulary, students can be asked to translate the incorrect options, or practise saying them to their partner or illustrating the key terms.

Outside a modern foreign languages (MFL) lesson, teachers can use the audio option with key vocabulary and short responses.

Q. What is the correct term to describe the number of people living in a specific location?

a   Economy

b   Population

c   Demographic

Reading questions and options aloud does take longer, but it can be a helpful approach for younger learners (especially if they do not possess the reading skills to comprehend the questions). Students with SEND and EAL could also benefit from hearing the spoken words.

If this is not ideal for most of the class, but individual learners will benefit from hearing the questions and options, there are digital tools that can contain text to speech/audio tools. Students can wear headphones to listen to the audio multiple-choice questions.

Multiple-Choice Questions and Feedback Techniques

There is absolutely no need for teachers to individually mark multiple-choice questions (the only exception to this is if the multiple-choice questions were part of a summative assessment task). There are several ways teachers can provide feedback; some techniques are more appropriate and effective than others.

If using an online quizzing tool, app, or website it is highly likely the technology will provide the feedback to learners instantly. The teacher will need to ensure students engage with that feedback, not just focusing on their scores, but also gaining an understanding of what they know and don't know yet. Online quizzing can be used outside the lesson as a home-learning task or to support independent study; an example of this is Seneca Learning™ or Sparx Maths™. This enables students to receive real-time feedback outside a lesson, without the need for teacher input.

Within a lesson, I would recommend teachers provide whole-class feedback, presenting the correct answers to the class and using this opportunity to discuss any mistakes, misconceptions, or probe for further checking for understanding. As the teacher is providing the correct answer (I would do so one at a time, not all at once) the students should self-assess their responses. They can do this easily with a tick or cross and, if needed, they can write the correct response alongside their initial incorrect answer. This is better than using peer assessment because it allows the learner to see for themselves how they performed on each question. In terms of retrieval practice, it should always be low stakes; peer assessment can increase the stakes, pressure and level of competition amongst students.

NOTE THIS DOWN

Have you experienced any challenges/issues/frustrations with multiple-choice questions?

....

....

What do you think are the main benefits and arguments for using multiple-choice questions?

....

....

How could you use a variation of multiple-choice questions in your classroom?

....

....

What online tools do you use or plan to use to support multiple-choice question design, creation and/or implementation?

....

....

CHAPTER 6
QUESTIONING
MIX IT UP!

This chapter covers:

- An explanation as to why teachers shouldn't solely rely on one questioning technique in the classroom
- A range of practical questioning techniques
- The importance of regularly reviewing and reflecting on questioning in your classroom.

VARIED QUESTIONING IN THE CLASSROOM

As discussed in the first chapter, there can be varied reasons and motivations for asking students questions in a lesson. Questions could be asked to check for understanding, or as an opportunity for retrieval practice. Questions can be asked to students verbally, through text or a digital format. Questions can be posed to the whole class, groups, pairs, or individuals. The classroom context is always key.

It is useful for the teacher to have a range of questioning techniques in their teaching toolkit that they can implement in the classroom. The teacher can decide which technique is the most appropriate or most likely to be effective. Not only can this be more interesting for learners, but it can also help to develop and assess different skills and increase student participation.

This chapter contains a range of questioning techniques. Each technique description contains a summary followed by a discussion of the key benefits, practical tips for implementation in the classroom and other points worth considering including potential problems, with suggested solutions.

TECHNIQUE: THINK–PAIR–SHARE

Summary: *Think–pair–share* is a straightforward yet potentially powerful questioning technique. It enables students to think individually about a question, problem or statement, followed by time to discuss their response and thoughts with a partner. The final stage involves sharing responses as a whole class. Think–pair–share can be used in combination with other questioning techniques, such as mini white boards, cold calling and choral response.

Benefits: This questioning technique can help develop a range of oracy skills, most notably listening and communication. It can help to develop social skills by providing opportunities for structured interaction within a lesson, with a focus on learning. This questioning technique ensures learners have sufficient time to consider and prepare an answer prior to sharing with the whole class.

Practical Tips: Think–Pair–Share

- When creating a seating plan for the class it is important to consider this questioning technique, as it requires learners to engage and communicate with the person sitting near or next to them. Seating plans can help teachers to avoid situations where conflict can arise, or a lack of engagement.
- Think–pair–share can be used for closed questions, where students are instructed to quickly compare their answers using *check, confirm or challenge*.
- Providing students with statements encourages wider debate and discussion during think–pair–share. Students can agree or disagree, as well as provide examples and counter-examples.

Potential Problems and Solutions: Think–Pair–Share

'How do you ensure the think time is not wasted?'

Jones and Wiliam (2021) advise teachers not to 'skimp on the think', but the challenges teachers face include knowing what students are thinking about. Other problems at the think stage include knowing how much time to provide and how to maintain student focus and attention. A solution to these potential problems can be to ask students to write down their responses (in their books or on mini whiteboards).

Writing down responses also supports students with the limitations of working memory, so that they have a written record to refer to when they are ready to share their response with their partner. This is known as *cognitive offloading*.

> 'How do you ensure students aren't having a social conversation (not related to the learning)?'

The teacher can circulate the classroom as students are discussing their answers, but it is exceedingly difficult (or impossible) for the teacher to listen to every conversation at once.

There are several solutions the teacher can consider. The first is to remind students of the rules, routines and expectations with this type of task. Accountability techniques can be employed. The teacher can hold students to account in the next stage by asking students what their partner told them. For example, 'William, did you agree with the answer Charlie provided?' or 'Ella, can you tell us what Isla told you?' Another method to structure the conversation is to label students 1 and 2. Person 1 talks when instructed and they are given a set amount of time. Their partner (person 2) must listen and not interrupt. On the instruction of the teacher, the students swap roles. This prevents one student dominating the conversation, ensures both participate and stresses the importance of listening to one another.

TECHNIQUE: MINI WHITE BOARDS

Summary: The mini white board (whether it's a dry-erase board, with pens and erasers, or a digital device acting as a direct substitute) is a mighty teaching and learning tool. Mini white boards, also referred to as Show-me™ boards, are a versatile, low-stakes tool that ensures every learner is responding to the question(s) asked. A teacher poses a question or problem to the class and each student writes their answer on a mini white board.

Benefits: The main benefit of this questioning technique is that it enables the teacher to see every single response (in contrast to only some individuals that have volunteered to answer). The teacher can then provide instant whole-class feedback. The mini white boards can help identify misconceptions or gaps in knowledge in real time, enabling the teacher to respond appropriately. The boards can also serve other purposes – for example, writing down ideas, thoughts and working out as a form of cognitive offloading. They can easily be combined with other questioning techniques.

Bruce Robertson, author and headteacher, writes (2021, p. 139):

'I believe that Show-me boards and great teaching go hand in hand. They are an invaluable formative assessment resource, and every teacher should have a class set.'

He adds:

'Teaching in this way not only makes students' thinking visible to you, but potentially to every other student in the room.'

Practical Tips: Mini White Boards

- Short answers lend themselves well to mini whiteboards, which make it easier and quicker for the teacher to read all responses and ask students to expand on their original response, if needed, with explanation and elaboration.

- Multiple-choice questions can work very well with mini white boards. Students can write a, b or c to represent their chosen answer.
- If students do not know the answer, there are several options, including having a go/guessing or drawing a large question mark on the board to let the teacher know there is a gap in their knowledge or something they would like help with.

Potential Problems and Solutions: Mini White Boards

> *'How do you stop students writing or drawing inappropriate or irrelevant content on the boards?'*

There are different ways to tackle this. It is essential that students are explicitly told how and when to use the mini white boards. Slick routines with the boards or devices can contribute to their effectiveness. It is worth spending time to explain expectations, with regular reminders provided.

> *'How do you stop students copying their peers' answers?'*

This can be another common occurrence, with students copying responses from their peers, especially if their answer is visible for others to see before they have responded. A simple strategy involves instructing all learners to show their boards at the same time with '1–2–3, show me!' or asking for one row at a time.

TECHNIQUE: IS THERE ANOTHER WAY/ANOTHER ANSWER?

Summary: This question is interesting because it asks students to consider other answers, reasons, or methods. Below is an example of this questioning technique in a history lesson:

Teacher   *What was the main cause of the outbreak of World War I?*

Student A   *The assassination of Franz Ferdinand, by Gavrilo Princip and the Black Hand Gang, was the main cause because it was this event that led to the announcement of war, a month later in 1914.*

Teacher   *The assassination was a compelling cause, the main cause like you suggested, but is there another answer? Another interpretation?*

Student B   *It could be argued that it was the role of the alliances that caused the outbreak of war. The assassination was a turning-point event, but that would not have caused the war without the reaction and involvement of the allies.*

Benefits: This questioning technique encourages students to consider other viewpoints, arguments and pieces of information. This can also be applied with a process or method when there are multiple ways to do or achieve something.

Practical Tips: Is there Another Way/Another Answer?

- This can be combined with think–pair–share, where students are required to discuss viable alternative answers with their partner.
- This could be used as a reflective method, after a task has been completed. Was there another way the same outcome could have been achieved? If so, how?

Potential Problems and Solutions: Is there Another Way/Another Answer?

> 'This doesn't work in some subjects where there is one concrete answer (no other possible correct responses).'

Although there could be one definitive answer, there could be different ways to solve the problem or reach the correct answer; this can be worth sharing and exploring. As with any questioning technique, if it isn't fit for purpose in a specific classroom context then it is not worth trying to find a way to implement it; instead focus on other techniques.

TECHNIQUE: WHAT'S MISSING?

Summary: Students are presented with curriculum material, and they must answer the question: *what's missing?* It could be a fill in the blank task or there could be a missing part of a diagram, or a label(s) removed from a diagram. There could be a missing keyword, a missing number, absent ingredient or piece of equipment or part of a process missing. For example, a paragraph could be provided without any punctuation; students would have to add the capital letters, commas, full stops and any other missing conventions. This questioning technique can be combined with other techniques.

Below are some examples across different subjects:

English literature: '*He hath a wisdom that doth . . . . . .*'
What's the missing part of the quote from Macbeth?

Food and nutrition: BMI = weight (kg)

?

What's missing from the BMI calculation method?

Maths: $4 \times ? = 16$
What is the missing number?

RE: . . . . . is the name of the place of worship in Judaism.
What is the missing key term?

Benefits: This is a flexible questioning technique that provides the learner with relevant context, with a key piece of information missing. This questioning technique can require learners to think hard and solve a problem.

Practical Tips: What's Missing?

- It's important to think carefully about which piece of information or section to remove. It should be central to the learning, but not obviously missing – so there is still a level of challenge.
- Students can create their own 'what's missing?' task using a piece of text, their class notes or a knowledge organiser. This can then be used for pair quizzing.
- After students have attempted the question, the completed text or image can be presented to the whole class and learners can self-assess their responses.

Potential Problems and Solutions: What's Missing?

'How do you ensure this type of question isn't too easy for learners?'

The amount that is missing can vary. It can be one word, or several words. The teacher can decide how much to hide/reveal based on the appropriate level of challenge.

TECHNIQUE: 'TELL ME MORE!'

Summary: There are different versions of this, but it's about digging deeper and getting more information from students. This can be in the form of probing questions, asking for examples and evidence, or simply going beyond their original response. This technique can be combined with other questioning techniques such as mini whiteboards and cold calling.

The drama example in Table 6.1 requires students to answer the question in the first column; the second column (this can be optional or compulsory) asks for more relevant information.

Table 6.1 An example of a 'tell me more' question

Question	Answer	Tell me more …
What is the role of a lighting designer?	*The lighting designer is responsible for the lighting throughout a performance*	*The lighting designer is an important behind-the-scenes role at the theatre. Lighting can be used to create mood, atmosphere and tension. They work closely with the director to enhance the overall performance of the play*

Tom Sherrington (2018) encourages teachers to ask students to 'say it again, better'. Sherrington writes:

> 'It's normal for first responses to be half-formed as students think aloud and formulate ideas. A second opportunity to respond allows them to finesse their answers, adding depth, accuracy, and sophistication. It's important not to inhibit students when they are unsure; it's also important not to allow them to assume mediocre answers are good enough.'

Benefits: This approach to questioning demonstrates high expectations as it goes beyond accepting students' first response. It encourages learners to extend their thinking and develop their initial answer.

Practical Tips: 'Tell Me More!'

- Students can use the *ABC model* to extend their discussions. The ABC model consists of asking learners what they *agree* with, what they can *build* upon and whether there is anything about their partner's response they can *challenge*.
- Students can write down the answer on a mini whiteboard; the teacher can call on individuals to elaborate and extend their response.

Potential Problems and Solutions: 'Tell Me More!'

> 'What if students struggle to add more to their answer?'

Students can be provided with extra time, so they are not rushed or under pressure to flesh out their answer. Another option could be to allow students to use their class notes or knowledge organiser as a prompt to add more to their original answer. Students can also be tasked to collaborate with other learners to generate more information together.

TECHNIQUE: QUESTION TIME

Summary: There are diverse ways this can be implemented and adapted in the classroom, but the premise is to provide specific time and instruction for students to prepare and ask questions. The questions the students ask can be for the teacher or their peers. The questions can focus on enhancing subject knowledge or they could be linked to feedback, performance and progression.

Benefits: As mentioned in Chapter 1, the questions are usually asked by the teacher, but encouraging students to ask questions can foster curiosity, enabling reflection and metacognitive awareness. The questions can provide useful insight for the teacher in terms of how they can support their learners moving forward, as well as identifying areas of interest for students.

Practical Tips: Question Time

- To give students plenty of time to prepare questions for question time, this could be part of a homework task, or they could be told this will take place in the next lesson.
- There are separate ways students can submit their questions. It could be open to volunteers to share with the class; alternatively, questions on a Post-it™ note or online tools such as Mentimeter.com™ allow students to submit a question or response anonymously.

- Students can be instructed to find the answer for themselves if the question is content-based. They can use textbooks, the internet or speak to other people as part of their research to find the answer(s) to their question(s).
- The teacher could present three questions to the class; using a show of hands, mini white boards or a digital device students can vote on which question they wish to know the answer to. This can be fun, promote curiosity and deepen subject knowledge.

Potential Problems and Solutions: Question Time

'Students often ask questions that they should already know the answer to.'

This can be one of the key rules and guidance for students with question time – to avoid wasting time. There is a difference between students asking a question they already know the answer to because they are struggling to think of a question to ask, and students asking a question because although they should know the answer, they don't. Question time can be very revealing for the teacher.

'Students don't always ask questions that are relevant to their learning.'

Students can be given sentence starters to help them say/write their question, as shown in Table 6.2. Gen AI can be used to create question stems, or these can be created by the teacher.

Table 6.2 Example of question time questions

Can you explain	I don't understand ...... yet. Can you help me?	I don't know how to .... Can you show me?
What does this ..... mean?	What is the difference between ___ and ___?	I think this ..... Is this correct?
Why is this ...... important?	What is the most important ....?	How can I get better at ...?

Learners can be instructed to generate a question linked to something specific and concrete, so they are unable to deviate from the lesson or curriculum content, or anything not linked to their learning.

Whilst there is a wide range of questioning techniques presented in this *Little Guide*, I am not advocating that teachers try every single one. Some questioning techniques lend themselves well to maths, whereas others work better in MFL or a practical-based subject. The age of the learners, prior knowledge of curriculum content and the goals within a lesson all influence the decisions teachers make.

Every questioning technique will have its limitations therefore identifying which questioning technique to no longer use is also a powerful reflection to act on. It is for the teacher to trial and reflect, stick, or ditch! Recognising a teaching technique is not suitable for a specific class, subject or topic is useful. Time and planning can then be directed to more successful questioning techniques. I hope teachers will read this *Little Guide* and be inspired to refine some of their existing questioning techniques and try a new one.

NOTE THIS DOWN

What are the most commonly used questioning techniques implemented in your classroom practice?

....

....

Are there any new questioning techniques you will use or a variation of an existing technique?

....

....

What are your key strengths with questioning in the classroom?

....

....

What are your areas for development with questioning in the classroom?

....

....

AFTERWORD

In education, fads and trends come and go. Revolutionary technologies have transformed some aspects of teaching, learning and assessment. But, alongside change there will always be continuity. Teacher and student relationships will always be important and feedback will always be required to move learning forward. Questioning will remain at the core of accessing curriculum content, will be used to ensure effective explanations and be central to formative and summative assessment design. Questioning techniques vary, but the fundamental principles are universal.

During the early years of my teaching career, I fell foul of common mistakes linked to questioning (many are explored throughout the various chapters of this *Little Guide*). Through honest feedback from colleagues, my own reflections, engaging with research literature and experiences, including observing others, I have developed a deeper understanding of questioning – in addition to enhancing my skills and confidence as a teacher and leader. I hope this book contributes to your professional development and practice, within the remit of questioning for teaching and learning.

REFERENCES

CHAPTER 1

Hattie, J. (2012) Know thy impact. *Educational Leadership*, 70(1), 18–23.

Wiliam, D. (2014) *The Right Questions, the Right Way*. Alexandria, VA: ASCD.

CHAPTER 2

Department for Education (DfE) (2025) *Generative Artificial Intelligence (AI) in Education*. June. Available at: www.gov.uk/government/publications/generative-artificial-intelligence-in-education/generative-artificial-intelligence-ai-in-education (accessed 17 July 2025).

CHAPTER 3

Lemov, D. (2021) *Teach Like a Champion 3.0: 63 Techniques that Put Students on the Path to College*. 3rd edition. San Francisco: Jossey-Bass, John Wiley & Sons.

McCrea, P. (2024) *Choral Response: Laying the Groundwork for Elaboration*. Available at: https://snacks.pepsmccrea.com/p/choral-response (accessed 17 July 2025).

Sherrington, T. (2022) Hands up! When it's helpful and when it's not. *teacherhead*. Available at: https://teacherhead.com/2022/11/06/hands-up-when-its-helpful-and-when-its-not/ (accessed 17 July 2025).

Yu, Y., Zhao, W., Li, A., Shanks, D. R., Hu, X., Luo, L. and Yang, C. (2025) Is covert retrieval an effective learning strategy? Is it as effective as overt retrieval? Answers from a meta-analytic review. *Educational Psychology Review*, 37, article no. 52.

CHAPTER 4

Agarwal, P. K., D'Antonio, L., Roediger, H. L. III, McDermott, K. B. and McDaniel, M. A. (2014) Classroom-based programs of retrieval practice reduce middle school and high school students' test anxiety. *Journal of Applied Research in Memory and Cognition*, 3(3), 131–9.

Bates, G. and Shea, J. (2024) Retrieval practice 'in the wild': teachers' reported use of retrieval practice in the classroom. *Mind, Brain, and Education*, 18(3), 249–57. doi: 10.1111/mbe.12420

Donoghue, G. M. and Hattie, J. A. C. (2021) A meta-analysis of ten learning techniques. *Frontiers in Education*, 6:581216. doi: 10.3389/feduc.2021.581216

Jones, K. (2021) *Retrieval Practice 2: Implementing, Embedding and Reflecting*. 1st edition. Suffolk: John Catt Educational.

Karpicke, J. D., Blunt, J. R. and Sumeracki, M. A. (2016) Positive effects of retrieval practice in elementary school children. *Frontiers in Psychology*, 7, 350. doi:10.3389/fpsyg.2016.00350

Monzon, N. and Hays, F. A. (2025) Leveraging generative artificial intelligence to improve motivation and retrieval in higher education learners. *JMIR Medical Education*, 11, e59210. doi: 10.2196/59210

Perry, T., Lea, R., Rübner Jørgensen, C., Cordingley, P., Shapiro, K. and Youdell, D. (2021) *Cognitive Science in the Classroom: Evidence and Practice Review*. London: Education Endowment Foundation.

Roediger, H. L. III, Putnam, A. C. and Smith, M. A. (2011) Ten benefits of testing and their applications to educational practice. In J. P. Mestre and B. H. Ross (eds), *Psychology of Learning and Motivation*, Vol. 55, pp. 1–36. San Diego, CA: Elsevier.

Tulving, E. and Thomson, D. M. (1973) Encoding specificity and retrieval processes in episodic memory. *Psychological Review*, 80(5), 352–73. Available at: https://doi.org/10.1037/h0020071 (accessed 17 July 2025).

CHAPTER 5

Jones, K. (2022) *Retrieval Practice Primary: A Guide for Primary Teachers and Leaders*. 1st edition. Suffolk: John Catt Educational.

CHAPTER 6

Jones, K. and Wiliam, D. (2021) *Getting the Think–Pair–Share Technique Right*. ASCD Educational Leadership blog. Available at: www.ascd.org/blogs/getting-the-think-pair-share-technique-right (accessed 17 July 2025).

Robertson, B. (2021) *The Teaching Delusion: 3. Power Up Your Pedagogy*. Suffolk: John Catt Educational.

Sherrington, T. (2018) Great teaching: the power of questioning. *teacherhead*. Available at: https://teacherhead.com/2018/08/24/great-teaching-the-power-of-questioning/ (accessed 17 July 2025).

INDEX

ABC (agree, build, challenge) model, 67
accuracy checks, in AI-generated content, 17
AI. *See* Generative Artificial Intelligence (Gen AI)
attention, focusing through questioning, 3–4
audio multiple-choice questions, 51–53

Bjork, Robert, 40

Carousel Learn™, 17
case study
   observing common questioning challenges, 30–31
   question banks across secondary department, 18–19
ChatGPT™, 16
choral response, 29–30
classroom management, 4
Classtools.net, 27
closed questions, 6
cognitive offloading, 60
cold calling, 25–27
confidence and motivation, questioning for, 3
confidence ratings, 49–50
consistency, as benefit of question banks, 14
contextual factors, subject-specific questioning, 5
covert retrieval practice, 28
cue cards, 40
cued recall, 39–40, 46
cue overload principle, 39
curiosity, questioning to spark, 2
curriculum planning, integration of retrieval practice, 38

Department for Education (DfE) guidance (2025), 17
digital quizzing apps, 7
digital vs. paper (question banks) formats, 17
Donoghue, Gregory, 37
dyslexia, 23

early career teachers (ECTs), support for, 15
Early Years Foundation Stage (EYFS) classroom, 5
EduCake™, 17
elaborate and extend (multiple-choice question) technique, 50–51
encoding specificity principle, 39
English as additional language learners (EAL)
   questioning support example, 23
   support with cued recall, 39
   text-to-speech tools, accessibility for, 53
   wait time and confidence, 8
evidence of learning, seeking, 2
exam preparation, and retrieval practice, 38

excitement, 2–3
exit ticket, 4, 46
external visitors, 16

fairness and bias, 28
flashcards, 15, 36, 40
free recall, 40–42

Generative Artificial Intelligence (Gen AI)
  creating multiple-choice quizzes, 48, 49
  creating question banks, 16–19
  support in creating recall tasks, 41–42
Goldilocks principle, and question difficulty, 6
Google Classroom™, 17
Google Gemini™, 16
"green light" technique, 24–25
guided vs. open recall, 41

hands up
  allowing, 26
  approach, 22
  choral response, 29–30
  cold calling, 25–27
  common questioning challenges (case study), 30–31
  for confirmation, 32
  "green light" technique, 24–25
  for ideas, 32
  pitfalls of, 31
  problems with, 22–24
  questioning, 7
  for questions, 32
  random name generators, 27–29
  to volunteer, 33
Hattie, John, 2, 37

impact awareness, questioning for, 2
inclusivity, 3, 22
independent study, multiple-choice feedback, 53
inspectors' use of question banks, 16
inspiration, questioning to provide, 2–3
instant whole-class feedback, 61
'is there another way/another answer?' technique
  benefits, 63
  example (World War I causes), 63
  practical tips, 63
  problems and solutions, 64

knowledge organisation and transfer, 37
knowledge organisers, 36, 49, 65, 68
'know thy impact', 2

learners
  engaging, 2–3
  questioning techniques to involve, 7
Lemov, Doug, 25
lesson planning, guided by questioning, 4
long-term memory, enhancement through retrieval, 28, 36
low-stakes quizzes, 36, 37

maths anxiety, student mindset and motivation, 23–24
McCrea, Peps, 29
Mentimeter.com™, 68
Microsoft Co-Pilot™, 16
mini white boards, 3, 4, 7, 15, 27, 49
  benefits, 61
  practical tips, 61

problems and solutions, 62
summary of method, 60
misconceptions, 5
modern foreign languages (MFL) lesson, 52
multiple-choice questions, xiii
    audio, 51–53
    confidence building role, 46
    confidence ratings, 49–50
    creation, 48–49
    design, 46–48
    different approaches to, 49
    digital vs. paper quizzes, 49
    elaborate and extend technique, 50–51
    extending, 49–54
    and feedback techniques, 53–54
    limitations of, 46
    mini white boards use in, 49, 62
    use in classroom, 46

non-specialist teachers, support for, 15

observation and reflection, 26
online question bank platforms, 17
online quizzing platforms, 17, 48, 49, 53
oracy, 4–5, 58
overt retrieval practice, 28

parental support, and question banks, 16
peer assessment, 54
peer observation, 26
"phone a friend" adaptation, 29
Plan it. Ask it. Be quiet., 9
planning questions, 9
plausible distractors, 48, 49
poorly designed questions, 8–9

Post-it™, 68
precise praise, building confidence, 24
pre-made question banks, 17
probing questions, 5
professional autonomy, 15
pronunciation and language learning, 29

quality assurance, 15, 18
question banks, xiii
    benefits of using, 14–16
    creating, 16–19
    cross-curricular access to, 19
    definition of, 14
    Gen AI tools, 16–19
    inclusion of answers in, 14
    across secondary department (case study), 18–19
questioning, xiii
    outcomes of, 2–3
    potential problems and solutions, 6–10
    purpose of, xiii, 2
    techniques to involve all learners, 7
    varied, 58
    See also specific entries
'question time' technique
    benefits, 68
    practical tips, 68–69
    problems and solutions, 69–70
    summary, 68
Quizizz™, 17, 48
Quizlet™, 17

random name generators, 27–29
recognition vs. recall, 46
reflection, questioning for, 3
reminders vs. retrieval practice, 36
retrieval practice, xiii

benefits of, 37
covert/overt, 28
cued recall, 39–40
curriculum design and planning, 38
definition of, 36
effectiveness of, 42
exam preparation and, 38
free recall, 40–42
keeping stakes low, 54
and multiple-choice questions, 46
positive effect, 37
providing opportunities for, 38–39
reminders vs., 36
retrieval strength, fluctuation of, 36, 38–39
revision strategies, 39
Robertson, Bruce, 61

scaffolded question design, 6–7
secondary department (case study), Key Stage 3 implementation, 18–19
self-assessment, 49, 53
Seneca Learning™, 53
Sherrington, Tom, 31–32, 66
Show-me™ boards. *See* mini white boards
spaced practice, 37, 38
Sparx Maths™, 53
special educational needs and disabilities (SEND)
  support with cued recall, 39
  text-to-speech tools, accessibility for, 53
  wait time and confidence, 8
spelling of key terms, 48
staff absence, cover support with question banks, 15
student feedback, 26

student questions, structuring and encouraging, 9–10
student use of question banks, 15
student voice, questioning to amplify, 3

Teach Like a Champion 3.0, (Lemov), 25
'Teleport Feature', 48
'tell me more!' technique
  benefits, 67
  example (drama – lighting designer), 66
  practical tips, 67
  problems and solutions, 67–68
  summary, 66–67
think–pair–share technique, 3, 24, 26
  benefits, 58–59
  practical tips, 59
  problems and solutions, 60
  summary of method, 58
timers and stopwatches, supporting wait time, 8

virtual learning environments (VLEs), 17
visual representation, of audio multiple-choice question, 52

wait and think time, 7–8
'what's missing?' technique
  benefits, 65
  practical tips, 65
  problems and solutions, 65–66
  summary with subject examples, 64–65
whole-class feedback, 53
Wiliam, Dylan, 9
workload reduction, through collaboration, 15, 18

www.ingramcontent.com/pod-product-compliance
Lightning Source LLC
Chambersburg PA
CBHW052212090526
44584CB00019BA/3069